You Can Quote Me On That

I0102212

Books by Cat Ellington

REVIEWS BY CAT ELLINGTON: THE COMPLETE
ANTHOLOGY, VOL. 1

REVIEWS BY CAT ELLINGTON: THE COMPLETE
ANTHOLOGY, VOL. 2

THE MAKING OF DUAL MANIA: FILMMAKING
CHICAGO STYLE

REVIEWS BY CAT ELLINGTON - THE COMPLETE
ANTHOLOGY LIMITED EDITION HOLIDAY GIFT
SET (BOOKS 1 & 2)

REVIEWS BY CAT ELLINGTON: THE COMPLETE
ANTHOLOGY, VOL. 3

MORE IMAGINATIVE THAN ORDINARY SPEECH:
THE POETRY OF CAT ELLINGTON

REVIEWS BY CAT ELLINGTON: A TRILOGY OF
UNIQUE CRITIQUES #1

MEMOIRS IN GOGYOHKA: A BOOK OF SHORT
POEMS AND MEMOIRS

YOU CAN QUOTE ME ON THAT: A COLLECTION
OF QUOTES BY CAT ELLINGTON

You Can Quote Me On That
A Collection of Quotes by Cat Ellington

Cat Ellington

Quill Pen Ink Publishing

THE BEAUTY OF EXPRESSION™

CHICAGO

PAPERBACK ISBN-13: 978-1-7334421-4-5

Library of Congress Control Number: 2022362737

Cover design: Tommie Mondell for Quill Pen Ink Publishing
Cover tint: Bumblebee
The Cat Ellington Literary Collection

Published by Quill Pen Ink Publishing
Chicago, Illinois, USA

Quill Pen Ink Publishing, 2020

Printed in the U.S.A.

Dedication

To Anita Sanders and Gary Martin—
For always believing in me

Preface

My dearest readers, I know what some of you may be thinking as you're reading this: *Seriously, Cat? Girl, did you (really) collect a whole bunch of your (own) quotes to put in a book?*

And my answer to you is, Yeah.

It may seem as though it's something new, but it's not. Books of this kind have been published for many years preceding it, and having read a few of them myself, you know, I found my inspiration.

I have been a professional in the creative arts for over twenty-five years now. But many of you have only been familiar with me for a few years because of the Internet. Joseph Strickland and I are both products of an old-era system that preceded the Internet Age. And during the extended time that we were out of professional service, we started a family, lived a "normal" life, laid low, and waited to be refueled in our respective fields and creative activities. However, by the time we resurfaced, the Internet and social media platforms were already up-and-running. And like so many others who came forth from the old brick-and-mortar era, we had to adjust to all of these new forms of technology.

It took some time, but we got used to it. And after a while, we went about the business of converting some of our physical creations to digital files, ergo, what you see today. In the process of building the Boutique Domain, which is my official website, I commenced conversing with my visitors (to whom I affectionately refer as my guests) about who I am and what I do. And as the days turned into weeks, which turned into months, and then into years, I realized that I'd had much to say. And a lot of what I had to say in the earlier days—via publications, databases, and weblogs—helped pave the way for this creative presentation.

Many words of wisdom have been shared throughout the history of Mankind by notable individuals in the public eye. And it pleases me to be able to pass along much of what I've learned in my own life—to not only those who will succeed me in this respect but also to those in the general public who will read my spoken words and gain a greater understanding about life.

The creation of *You Can Quote Me On That* was one fun-filled process! I swear, I had a ball going through old interviews, weblogs, books, and quotes databases to source my material. And I wouldn't take the time-consuming research back for anything. Indeed, I truly enjoyed composing this work. And I hope that you, my dear readers, will enjoy reading it just as much.

Finally, in honor of the book's creation, I thought it would be nice to introduce the effort in my unique way. Therefore, I opted to write my introduction page in seven structures of Tanka poetry to give it a bit of flair that differs from standard book introductions. And this, too, had been a lot of fun. God, I love an exciting challenge!

(Smiles)

Thank you, my dear readers, for your support of my work in literature. Please, have a good time with this one.

Acknowledgments

Thank you, Father God Almighty, for this blessed work that you, and you alone, have given me to do here on your Earth. Thank you for my life as well as for my well-being. And thank you for your divine guidance through it all: for here lies yet another dedication of which you are entirely worthy. I love you.

Thank you, Christ Jesus, for your infinite wisdom, knowledge, and understanding: for I am nothing at all if not humbled by it. I love you.

Thank you, glorious Holy Spirit, for your truth, love, mercy, and providence: for the first fruits of my praise shall forever be bestowed upon you. All my love.

Mr. Joseph Strickland, I love you, baby. Thank you for everything, even for every wise word you've spoken and every kind deed you've done. You're my partner for life.

Nathaniel, Nairobi, and Naras, I love you three so much it pierces my emotions. I am so proud of every one of you and to call you my children. Thank you all for your support. And thank you for deeming me 'The Best Mama Ever.'

Freddie, Maurice, Nicky, and Timbo, thank you all so much for being such a great blessing to my family over the years. You mean so much to me, every one of you. And I will never forget your love and kindness. Not ever. I love all of you.

And to all of my readers, I say thank you. Thank you for supporting my work in literature. I appreciate all of you.

Contents

Introduction

(In Seven Structures of Tanka)

Indeed, I've done it,
What composed a collection
Of my favorite quotes
For this enjoyable book
In (general) nonfiction.

My precious of days,
Over the last seven years
I've had much to say.
And I thought it would be fun
To get this unique work done.

Inspired by dreams
And other creative things,
I mated my pen
With my lonely sheet paper;
I succumbed to my Savior.

As He guided me,
I glided through the process
Of compilation—
Gathering quotes here and there
To build this presentation.

And here it is now,
Causing me nothing but wow—

Yes, to Him, I bow:
Indeed, I'm wholly honored
By another task conquered.

This— is how I feel:
Oceans of my emotions
Roll over in waves—
Rushing in truth and wisdom
In every creative phase.

I covered my ground
With a strut and witty quip,
Voicing my mindset—
I talk it like I walk it,
And you can quote me on that.

Introducing *You Can Quote Me On That: A Collection of Quotes by Cat Ellington*
I hope you all enjoy it!

Love always,

Cat Ellington

"I don't just dare, I quadruple dare."

—Cat Ellington

Quotes

1) "For the truth is what I represent. The truth is what I love. And the truth is what I choose to infuse into my creative contribution concerning the written word."
—**Cat Ellington**

2) "I do me and not anyone else. And I don't, and won't, allow myself to be defined by anyone else."
—**Cat Ellington**

3) "I will not 'water down' my concentrated efforts to appease anyone, nor will I sugarcoat the truth to make it more digestible to the one willing to shy away from it."
—**Cat Ellington**

4) "I love it when my creative juices begin to flow."
—**Cat Ellington**

5) "I bought my very first diary at a Chinatown basement store in 1982. And I've been recording day-by-day accounts about my life in them ever since."
—**Cat Ellington**

6) "It's always good to remember the past in order to understand both your present and future."
—**Cat Ellington**

7) "Whether you be Jews (according to the flesh) or Gentiles, respectively, have a healthy love for each and every one of yourselves, and get on out there and blaze your own trails. If you're holding down any fort, always rely on omnipotent spiritual support. If you're like me and possess a passion for the loveliest of fashion, hey, what the hell, wear it well! Always look at the glass half full, and don't take no muthafuckin' bull. My dearest men and women, in all that you do, make life a stone groove."
—**Cat Ellington**

8) "Live life to the fullest, laugh out loud, and love intensely. Be yourselves no matter where you are. And always look in front of you, not behind you. Go for it with all you have in you."
—**Cat Ellington**

9) "Memoirs in Gogyohka serves as the appetizer before the main course of my biographical accounts."
—**Cat Ellington**

10) "I love the South Side Community Art Center so much that I could literally move into it and live there for the rest of my natural life."
—**Cat Ellington**

11) "I prefer older men. That's right, older men. I like my men 'well-seasoned,' if you will, meaning with a little bit of 'salt and pepper' sprinkled in their hairy parts."
—**Cat Ellington**

12) "I love people wholeheartedly, but my quality of life is not dependent upon whether or not they like, love, or approve of me."
—**Cat Ellington**

13) "Basically, I bring the truth and the light through the written word: for in such a way am I utilized as a creative human vessel."
—**Cat Ellington**

14) "Songwriting cannot be taught, it is a God-given gift from the womb."
—**Cat Ellington**

15) "The ability to love is the ability to be free."
—**Cat Ellington**

16) "The first thing I look for, in addition to a performer's range, is a performer's look in comparison to the character. That is very important to me as a casting director."
—**Cat Ellington**

17) "I'm able to love others because I love myself. Period."
—**Cat Ellington**

18) "Diaries are very special record books, and I genuinely believe that everyone should have at least one (or maybe even two) in their possession."
—**Cat Ellington**

19) "Nearly everything I do is independent. It's my nature to be fiercely independent. And publishing my written works of literature under my own imprint—Quill Pen Ink Publishing—is no different."
—**Cat Ellington**

20) "After you have done your work—challenging as it may have been to complete—and release it in the marketplace, be not concerned with sales, reviews, critical acclaim, or anything else of the like. After you've written and published a book, you're now an AUTHOR. And that great honor can NEVER be taken away from you, no matter what."
—**Cat Ellington**

21) "Writing is my earthly calling. The world of words is the perfect utopia in whose rapture I am altogether caught up."
—**Cat Ellington**

22) "Men and women in the creative arts should be free to express themselves creatively without interference from those who are without honor where having talent is concerned."
—**Cat Ellington**

23) "As a working professional in the entertainment industry, I have come to truly cherish both my creative freedom and my independence. Because I, for one, know how precious and priceless they are."
—**Cat Ellington**

24) "For me as a writer, especially one who would be considered a prolific writer, the composition of words is somewhat therapeutic, deeply relaxing, fun-filled."
—**Cat Ellington**

25) "I have always told people, 'Should the words stop flowing, I'm done.'"
—**Cat Ellington**

26) "I am indeed my most unmerciful critic."
—**Cat Ellington**

27) "I have never thought of myself as being someone who would have fans."
—**Cat Ellington**

28) "Those men and women who may enjoy the work I do mean everything and then some to me. Because as a creative artist, particularly as a writer, I am a very emotional person. And I want them to feel—if only to a certain extent—what I feel as the earthly creator of the public works. I want to know that they appreciate all the hard work it takes to accomplish such works. The public at large will never fully understand the joy their appreciation gives the creative artist. Never will they. But I cherish every one of them. And I don't take any of them for granted. There is absolutely no place for underestimation here."
—**Cat Ellington**

29) "I'm not narcissistic or arrogant, I'm just terribly self-confident."
—**Cat Ellington**

30) "I started writing songs in 1981, and I wrote my very first book review in 1982."
—**Cat Ellington**

31) "I have many fitting monikers, and 'Statuesque Maverick' is indeed one of them."
—**Cat Ellington**

32) "Words are my second nature, a major part of my creative DNA, my dearest cohorts. And I feel empty, even lost, without them."
—**Cat Ellington**

33) "Stephen King is my 'Maine man.'"
—**Cat Ellington**

34) "I also have a number of other hobbies, including collecting charm bracelets. I swear, I am completely enamored with charm bracelets. In my personal opinion, they are a perfect representation of women: sexy, flirty, stylish, feminine, and unique. Much like with earrings, nail polish, and perfume, I feel deathly naked if I'm not wearing a charm bracelet."
—**Cat Ellington**

35) "My writing process? Ink pen and notebook; hand lotion and laptop; peace and quiet; coffee, Tazo tea, or Bigelow Vanilla Chai; keyboard and handheld recorder (if the work is to be musical); bubblegum and highlighter; research journal and, of course, a little inspiration. Give a gal these things and she's good to go."
—**Cat Ellington**

36) "I'll admit that I am a woman who is very hard to impress."
—**Cat Ellington**

37) "There are many, many inspirations behind the Cat Ellington song work, the Cat Ellington poem, the Cat Ellington review, and the Cat Ellington work of nonfiction."
—**Cat Ellington**

38) "With the Cat Ellington critique, there will always be something mentioned that will strongly engage the thought process, something educational that my readers will be able to gain great wisdom from."
—**Cat Ellington**

39) "I think that as long as there are authors writing books there will be book publishing entities (be they major or independent) in the business of distributing those works out into the marketplace for the public at large. Technology is ever-changing, sure, but no form of scientific knowledge, at least not in my own personal opinion, will ever stomp out the book publishing industry, just as no Internet outlet or social media platform will ever fully take the place of brick-and-mortar stores, print media businesses, movie theaters, bookstores, etc."
—**Cat Ellington**

40) "I rotate around the arts – chiefly in the music industry where I create, professionally, as a heterogeneous songwriter and music producer."

—**Cat Ellington**

41) "By now, it is widely known that I am in the habit of writing in title case; however, I try not to do so in my literary work."
—**Cat Ellington**

42) "The best advice I've ever heard is to make sure that I maintain creative control."
—**Cat Ellington**

43) "My favorite book of all time is the Holy Bible because it is the ultimate container of tremendous wisdom. And I love wisdom. I love absolutely everything about it."
—**Cat Ellington**

44) "I tend to write in title case, a habit of mine that most people would consider to be quite unusual. Such a style of writing has been all I've known for over thirty years, considering that I'm a songwriter. Because of that craft, I have, for far too long, been in the habit of writing in titles."
—**Cat Ellington**

45) "Roger Ebert inspires me in the review writing process, Stephen King inspires me in the classic suspense process, Iceberg Slim inspires me in the unfiltered process, Carl Hiaasen inspires me in the humor process, and Jackie Collins inspires me in the contemporary layout process."
—**Cat Ellington**

46) "There is no such thing as 'writer's block.' That's just a code term for anxiety. Sit down, brew a pot of coffee or a cup of tea, relax, clear your mind, meditate a minute or two, and the words will come. Writer's write. That's why they're called writers. The gift is already in them. They just need to guard their minds against all forms of anxiety."
—Cat Ellington

47) "Live life to the fullest, laugh out loud, and love intensely. Be yourselves no matter where ya may be, look in front of ya, not behind ya, and go for it with all you have in ya."
—Cat Ellington

48) "Allow peace to wrap itself around you, and be mightily blessed by the Best."
—Cat Ellington

49) "Enjoy your lives upon this Earth and put your great Creator first. Be at peace, be at ease, and don't tolerate no feeble knees. Stand up straight, walk by faith, and don't let no clowns jerk you around. When Satan gets ta hatin', rise above. When Satan gets ta hatin', stay in love."
—Cat Ellington

50) "When, while in pursuit of your dreams, you encounter doors being closed in your face, kindly knock again. And if those same doors refuse to reopen, kick those muthafuckas in, that you may cross each symbolic threshold and take aim

at staking your claim. Always remember that great faith will carry you a mighty long way."

—Cat Ellington

51) "Chicago. She's the greatest city in the world."
—Cat Ellington

52) "I had way too much fun writing Memoirs in Gogyohka, and I loathed to see the creative process on it come to an end."
—Cat Ellington

53) "My dream is to join ASCAP like all of the best songwriters and to have a star on the Walk of Fame in Hollywood like all of the great people."
—Cat Ellington in a diary entry excerpt from 1982

54) "While it's true that my father wasn't in the home (I was brought up by my single mother, God bless her), I have not set out to fill the void he left, I just desire mature men in relationships, that's all."
—Cat Ellington

55) "It's a universally known fact, what that girls are seven years ahead of boys on the maturity scale."
—Cat Ellington

56) "I've always loved people and genuinely believe that people have a right to connect with one another without having to worry about various forms of hatred in a society seeking to rip them apart."
—**Cat Ellington**

57) "I don't care whether you're well-known or unknown, rich or poor, overweight or emaciated, wearing shoes on your feet from the House of Louboutin or Payless, scented in Chanel N°5 or some Dollar Store fragrance, I'd be a true friend to you still. But if you show your ass on me, just out of spite, I'll tear your ass up with the truth."
—**Cat Ellington in response to Mariah Carey**

58) "My spirit is the kind that rebels against being controlled: for it strives to go against the grain rather than along with it."
—**Cat Ellington**

59) "I didn't need to be a man-pleaser, or a sycophant, or an ass-kisser, or a slave to men."
—**Cat Ellington**

60) "Where the gift of songwriting is concerned, the Lord has bestowed upon me a great wisdom in this particular craft."
—**Cat Ellington**

61) "I truly believe that people should strive to make love and not war."

—Cat Ellington

62) "I hate fear and ignorance—with everything I have in me—because they divide people."

—Cat Ellington

63) "Before anyone can respect another, they must first respect themselves. And before anyone can understand another, they must first understand themselves. That's common sense. But we don't see a lot of common sense being utilized in society. Instead, we play witness to the exact opposite."

—Cat Ellington

64) "I write whatever the Spirit moves me, or rather commands me, to write."

—Cat Ellington

65) "Whenever there arose in my life a unique situation worthy of a written testimonial, I took the opportunity to record my witness, pen to paper."

—Cat Ellington

66) "I love the craft of writing because it's therapeutic, y'know? There is simply no other physical gift in existence greater than that of writing. It is a magnificent gift that should be cherished and nurtured, but never trifled with or taken for granted."
—**Cat Ellington**

67) "Ignorance is not bliss and neither is the sorrow of the heart."
—**Cat Ellington**

68) "I do not stand in a place to present myself as anyone's judge as I am no better or greater than any other human being. We all fall short, even every one of us, because we're human."
—**Cat Ellington**

69) "To many in this present generation, people like myself are perceived differently – as if we're anomalies, enigmas, or offenders, if you please."
—**Cat Ellington**

70) "I, Cat Ellington, am not someone who conforms well. In fact, I have never been such an individual. It's just not in me."
—**Cat Ellington**

71) "Nothing in the world terrifies me more than to have the words stop coming. If I can't write, I could be of no use."
—**Cat Ellington**

72) "Songwriters are the architects of the music industry. Without a songwriter there could not, and would not, be a music industry. We create the blueprint."
—**Cat Ellington**

73) "I don't have haters, I have self-haters – people were already full of self-hatred way before they ever heard of a woman named Cat Ellington. Because such people have no faith and absolutely refuse to make God their trust. Period."
—**Cat Ellington**

74) "Contrary to popular belief, White people don't have a monopoly on the spirit of racism. That spirit is an equal opportunity troubler, even clawing at the minds of those African-American self-haters who find it difficult to accept that a Black woman, such as myself, could compose bluegrass or classical music. That is yet another example of racism."
—**Cat Ellington**

75) "Men are men, be they Jewish men or Gentile men. And I both respect and love them all equally. When it comes to my love life, I do not take into consideration race, creed, color, nationality, or origin, I just love and respect others as I do myself."
—**Cat Ellington**

76) "Women. They can never get ahead in life because they're too damn busy holding one another back and clawing each other up."
—**Cat Ellington**

77) "There is no such person as a 'nobody.' For every man (and every woman) having been made by the hand of the Lord thy God, even in His image, is somebody."
—**Cat Ellington**

78) "Make life a stone groove."
—**Cat Ellington**

79) "Gifts, talents, the Lord has given every one whom He has created and allowed to live here on His Earth, including myself, some kind of a gift or talent."
—**Cat Ellington**

80) "I will not ever bring a testimony that I can't and won't back up. I'm not a perfect individual, but honesty is my way. And it's the only way I know, even if I am in show business."
—**Cat Ellington**

81) "Someone once told me that women are catty. And it's true, they are. But not one of them is cattier than myself; hence my nickname, Cat: for the same has been given to me for a legitimate reason."
—Cat Ellington

82) "Having been born a free spirit, there is no one with whom I can't get along. Just ask anyone who knows me, and they'll tell you the same."
—Cat Ellington

83) "Wisdom is lovely in all her array. And people ought to allow themselves to embrace her while they have a chance. Because once people learn to love themselves, it will be quite easy for them to love others."
—Cat Ellington

84) "I don't bother anybody and I expect to be left alone."
—Cat Ellington

85) "Life is worth living, but not dying for; and strength speaks volumes in individualism, not in groups. Hope will carry you to a land flowing with great opportunities, and faith will establish you there."
—Cat Ellington

86) "Despite much opposition that one may be subjected to in the world, or the many trials that one might undergo in the world, the Lord God Almighty still takes care of his own and causes great favor to be bestowed upon his own – to let the people know that he, and he alone, is in control and absolutely no one else, be they spiritual beings or human beings."
—**Cat Ellington**

87) "Every form of music that one hears in every society was composed by a songwriter, yet we're the most disrespected in the industry, and the most looked down on. But without us, none of it could or would be. The craft of songwriting requires great skill and a lot of hard work and dedication; therefore, songwriters are worthy of a little more respect."
—**Cat Ellington**

88) "There's just somethin' about the feline kind, baby. There's just somethin' about the feline kind."
—**Cat Ellington**

89) "If my only creative hat was that of songwriting, say in only a genre or two, then some people would probably never hear of me as I would be a bit more obscure."
—**Cat Ellington**

90) "I do my job and I mind my own business. But when there is someone else constantly in my business and being an evil trial to me, then that has to be addressed."

—Cat Ellington

91) "I work in show business and we tend to have egos to some degree or other."
—**Cat Ellington**

92) "So many people want to act like they don't know who Cat Ellington is, but I know good and damn well they do."
—**Cat Ellington**

93) "When Father God designed my creative coat, he didn't intend for it to fit anyone but me."
—**Cat Ellington**

94) "No one has a monopoly on anything. We are all inspired by something or someone."
—**Cat Ellington**

95) "There ain't a man or a woman on Earth who can accuse me, Cat Ellington, of being envious, or jealous-hearted, or a 'hater,' and be telling the truth."
—**Cat Ellington**

96) "I'm the first person who would build somebody up if God gave them great talents and abilities. I would be among the first to lavish them with compliments. Envy towards others is not my trial."
—**Cat Ellington**

97) "I happen to love me, not in an arrogant or vain sense, but rather in a spirit of truth."
—**Cat Ellington**

98) "Be yourself and learn to love yourself, then others will be able to truly love you."
—**Cat Ellington**

99) "I don't have a problem with anyone finding inspiration in anything that I do, because I also have those who inspire me in many ways."
—**Cat Ellington**

100) "Mariah Carey is my number one fan."
—**Cat Ellington**

101) "I don't bite or scratch. I purr, hecky yeah, but I don't bite or scratch."
—Cat Ellington

102) "I absolutely love all things feminine, elegant, exquisite, lovely, and beautiful."
—Cat Ellington

103) "I don't go through life making enemies. I'm at peace with those who are at peace with me. And in most cases, even with those who are not."
—Cat Ellington

104) "I have nothing to lose where you're concerned. If push comes to shove, I'll just turn and walk away from it. Because by the grace of Father God Almighty, I was Cat Ellington doing what I do before he allowed you to bring yours into being on this Earth of his, and I'll still be Cat Ellington doing what I do should he command for yours to be removed from off the face of his Earth today or tomorrow."
—Cat Ellington in response to a certain Twitter executive

105) "The Boutique Domain was chosen to be considerable in its existence because its purpose is to serve all of my creative divisions."
—Cat Ellington

106) "I am the *only* Cat Ellington in the craft of songwriting."
—**Cat Ellington**

107) "Once a person finds his or her way onto my heart's soft spot list, they remain there on it forever, no matter what."
—**Cat Ellington**

108) "The Sweet Smell of Success is an excellent film! Nothing short of extraordinary is this film! Phenomenal. Absolutely phenomenal!"
—**Cat Ellington**

109) "I hate to have my honesty and my integrity doubted or questioned. I hate that shit."
—**Cat Ellington**

110) "If people come at me crooked like snakes, I will cut them verbally and then pay their rent or mortgage afterward if the Spirit moves me to. That's just my way. But deliberately doing or saying anything that will cause them to feel pain, shame, or ridiculed, is not."
—**Cat Ellington**

111) "I'm a fairly casual gal, ya know? I enjoy the simple things in life, like my bootcut jeans and my low top Converse All Stars."
—**Cat Ellington**

112) "Make love like banshees. It's a good calorie burner, ya know?"
—**Cat Ellington**

113) "I would never quit on a book, even if it's awful. Once I start something, I believe in finishing it. The process of completing such a book will take me much longer, but I wouldn't abandon it altogether."
—**Cat Ellington**

114) "I'll have you know that I am a woman who is not ashamed of anything where those whom I love, care deeply for, and have a great fondness of, are concerned. It doesn't matter to me if those about whom I care work as fry cooks or dishwashers in fast food restaurants earning minimum wage, or in the tech industry earning millions or billions of dollars in stock options and salary, when I love, I love strong, I love hard, I love truthfully, and I love unconditionally."
—**Cat Ellington**

115) "My bustline and hips are genuine, as is my waistline. I have never had any plastic surgical procedure performed on my person. Ever."
—**Cat Ellington**

116) "I don't feel any differently now than I did when I had been a member of the general public."
—Cat Ellington on being a public figure

117) "I can't write when I'm running on emotions. Because if I'm writing while running on emotions, I'm gonna be fuckin' up my punctuation and everything. I'm a very sloppy writer when I'm emotional."
—Cat Ellington

118) "I may feel like an everyday woman, but I am no longer an everyday woman. Once that line was crossed, I couldn't go back. I'm known for what I do now. My life of anonymity is now gone forever."
—Cat Ellington on being a public figure

119) "I wouldn't ever have a roof over my head, even if it were a shack, where you and your beautiful babies couldn't come and lay your three heads or make yourselves welcome to the food and drinks therein, but if you pull a diva out of your ass on me, I'll rip you up with the truth."
—Cat Ellington in response to Mariah Carey

120) "The only thing worse than a self-hating heterosexual woman is a self-hating lesbian."
—Cat Ellington

121) "The truth is that I love being a woman, and feeling like a woman, and looking like a woman, and smelling like a woman, and engaging like a woman. And only the loins of the male species can conjure the full invincibility of my womanliness."
—**Cat Ellington**

122) "I don't need to hide behind fake accounts to indirectly communicate with anyone. If there is someone with whom I am interested in connecting, trust that I will be straightforward in my approach. Because whoever he or she may be, they have a right to know who it is reaching out to them, especially if they're public figures."
—**Cat Ellington**

123) "We are not one another's enemies, but we have one common enemy. And his name is Satan."
—**Cat Ellington**

124) "When people refuse to acknowledge the Lord God and they strut about the Earth void of faith and spiritual understanding, they become wide open, albeit empty, wells for Satan to fill up."
—**Cat Ellington**

125) "The Spirit of Truth speaking in the ears of one who is tempted to love a lie is like a bucket of ice-cold water being thrown on one who sleeps naked."
—**Cat Ellington**

126) "According to many of them, I should be cast in society as a maid. According to many of them, I should be a so-called 'Welfare Queen' struggling to make ends meet. According to many of them, I should be working a back-breaking job making barely enough to survive. According to many of them, I should be a big, fat, loud, and sloppy cow who knows her place—and who stays in it—at the bottom of the 'Totem Pole' in society. According to many of them, I should be bleaching my skin, coloring my hair a bright shade of yellow, wearing light-colored contacts, and mimicking the standard valley girl, all to pledge my allegiance to the White Caste System in society."
—Cat Ellington

127) "When many people in the world see a Black woman like myself, it confuses them."
—Cat Ellington

128) "Now am I an unforgiving person? No, not at all; I'm just not going to allow anyone to kick me twice after they've already enjoyed the pleasure of kicking me once lest my hand should be forced to inflict upon them severe harm."
—Cat Ellington

129) "A lotta people don't wanna fight for me, so I always fight for myself. And I win, too. All I have to do is sit on them."
—An 11-year-old Cat Ellington on her struggle with childhood obesity

130) "To cherish every day of life is wisdom, and to nurture that life is understanding. Because the next second, minute, hour, day, week, month, or year, is not promised to any of us; therefore, I've learned not to take anyone in my life for granted ever again, and to love them just a little bit more."
—**Cat Ellington**

131) "I'm one of those types of people who love to see the wicked get back what they put out. And there is absolutely nothing wrong with that. The Lord doesn't hold a passion for truth and justice against anyone."
—**Cat Ellington**

132) "One day we'll find that old peace that we lost as a people of one heart, one mind, and one body. One day our children will again be free to stay out late and play for as long as they like without having to fear stray bullets ('with no names'), or the destroyer that does not come except to stir up strife and chaos in our communities. One day, by the grace of God, we, as a people, will be made whole again."
—**Cat Ellington on Chicago's South Side**

133) "Once upon a time, I used to feel so self-conscious about my height, especially when I was a younger girl, because I was tall for my age."
—**Cat Ellington**

134) "Someone once said to me, 'The weak hate the strong; Hyenas hate lions.' And to that, I said 'Amen!'"
—**Cat Ellington**

135) "The South Side of Chicago is my oyster. It always has been and it always will be: for I am profoundly proud of both it and its people."
—**Cat Ellington**

136) "Any woman can look her best if she feels her best. And anyone can have material things if they work hard enough to obtain them."
—**Cat Ellington**

137) "Before, people detested me because I was a despicable fatso; now they detest me because I am the complete opposite of a despicable fatso. And that's the Lord's doing. The Lord stopped their heads from wagging at me a long time ago, and He shut up their mouths from laughing at me a long time ago."
—**Cat Ellington**

138) "My guess is that many of these so-called Millennials have always been lazy as the word itself, but their shortcomings were hidden by the obscurity they dwelled in before the creation of social media."
—**Cat Ellington**

139) "It makes me sick to my stomach to see certain people being referred to as 'Web stars' or 'Internet famous,' because such people are nearly always without merit."
—**Cat Ellington**

140) "Too many women have forgotten themselves, striving to take the places of men in every aspect of society. And they too will fail because God made the woman from the rib of the man, not the man from the rib of the woman; therefore, the woman is the weaker vessel."
—**Cat Ellington**

141) "A woman cannot do everything a man does, it just doesn't work that way. And those women out there in the world, the same women who are being tempted to covet power and having power over men, will not only destroy themselves but also their daughters."
—**Cat Ellington**

142) "In all of my years, even since the time that I was old enough to understand, I ain't ever seen a failed hustler, or a survivor begging bread. And every man and woman on this Earth with a success story to tell can be counted among such."
—**Cat Ellington**

143) "I am the most interesting woman in the world."
—**Cat Ellington**

144) "No one can bring a charge of hostile treatment against me and be witnessing truthfully. Not even one. Not the well-known public figures who have achieved fame, and not any of those who are members of the general public. Not even one."
—**Cat Ellington**

145) "If I ever approach you, I won't ever approach you crooked like a snake; but when I approach you, I'm gonna approach you straight. If I owe you a dollar bill, I'm not gonna pay you back 99 cents, I'm gonna pay you back the whole dollar, not a penny short. And if all I have in my piggy bank is five thousand dollars, I'm not gonna tell you I

got ten thousand when I know good and damn well all I got is five thousand. If I tell you that I'ma give you a loaf of bread, I'm not gon' dishonor my word and part ways with only a slice, you're gonna get the whole loaf."

—Cat Ellington

146) "I love my city but I hate the godless ways of many of her children – all of whom include both the Jew and the Gentile."
—**Cat Ellington on Chicago**

147) "No matter who you are—Jew or Gentile, well-known or unknown, rich and wealthy or poor and needy—if you find that you're constantly the target of unprovoked animosity from many people in the world, be they familiar persons or strangers, there is a good chance you're being called, and the spirits in the world can detect the 'light' within you."
—**Cat Ellington**

148) "No true love can exist unless God is involved. Because wherever Satan is, hatred and all manner of chaos will most certainly be there alongside him. But not real love. Never that."
—**Cat Ellington**

149) "I would rather be hated by the world for being an obedient Pentecostal Christian woman—particularly an African-American woman of the Pentecostal Christian faith—than a lost soul in the world system falsely loved—and *accepted*—by a bunch of strangers for being a practicing sinner."
—**Cat Ellington**

150) "They did not make me, therefore, they cannot break me."

—Cat Ellington

151) "I must admit, I utterly hate the idea of anyone trying to control me. Seriously, just the thought of it kindles a wave of burning anger within me. I don't like being controlled by other people. Period."
—**Cat Ellington**

152) "I am from the South Side of Chicago, even from its innermost parts. And there ain't a man or a woman alive—be he or she gay or straight—who can say *anything* that's going to shock me. Neither is there even one who can out-cuss me, or brandish a verbal sword bearing a double edge sharper than that of my own."
—**Cat Ellington**

153) "I was being raised by a bunch of hell-raising, and wig-snatching, 'dykes' and 'fairies' on Chicago's South Side way before being homosexual became a semi-acceptable, and somewhat celebrated, lifestyle in current society."
—**Cat Ellington**

154) "I, Cat Ellington, was the original fag hag. I was the first person to ever use the term in 1989, though I have never received any credit for it – being as that I had only been a member of the general public during that era and not yet a public figure in any branch of the arts."
—**Cat Ellington**

155) "My lips don't do ass. They never have, and I don't reckon that they soon ever will. I am who I am—take me or leave me."

—Cat Ellington

156) "I will continue doing my Lord's work as a creative artist in the arts & entertainment industry. And know for a certainty, that not even one will be allowed to shoo me away as a result of their being 'offended' by the hue of my flesh and/or by the Spirit of Truth who dwells within me: for I have come from a long line of fighters and I intend to stand my ground."
—**Cat Ellington**

157) "I am not tempted to believe myself as being better than—or as good as—anyone else. I just like my coffee the way I like my coffee: sometimes black, sometimes creamy, but always sweet."
—**Cat Ellington**

158) "False fame is lazy, without honor, and seeks its own kind with which to associate. But true fame—and the legitimate recognition it inevitably brings—is partial to those whose hands have toiled long and hard in his or her respective fields and/or crafts."
—**Cat Ellington**

159) "No one has ever been able to defeat spiritual forces with a carnal mind. To obtain victory in spiritual warfare, one must battle back with a spiritual mind."
—**Cat Ellington**

160) "Women are paying big money—even going broke—for vanity purposes, desperate to look like someone else whom they are not. Because of the demons called

self-hatred, low self-esteem, envy, jealousy, and covetousness."

—Cat Ellington

161) "Simply telling people to just love themselves and to just be themselves is always easier said than done. Because the weapons of spiritual warfare in many peoples' minds have pierced too deep for far too long. And it's going to take divine intervention to free them from their enslavement."
—**Cat Ellington**

162) "God created beauty, not ugliness. And it will be well for you to understand that you are a magnificent and unique beauty—whomever you may be."
—**Cat Ellington**

163) "I am not a perfect individual by any measure, and I've never presented myself as such. I'll be the first one to testify about my flaws—physical or otherwise—without shame."
—**Cat Ellington**

164) "As human beings, we all fall short. Not one of us gets it just right all the time, and it is for a certainty that none of us ever will."
—**Cat Ellington**

165) "Father God sent every original song work, covering 24 genres, to me over the course of 35 years. I didn't make them up or engage in what is fraudulent, infringement, or plagiarism. Each and every lyric and chord are His, not mine, I'm just the human vessel being greatly used. And I'm beyond humble because He could've chosen anyone else to bestow His blessing upon. But He chose to use me in this particular craft, that the works may be a blessing to many

people around the world, that I may receive great honor from Him through the works, and that His awesome name would be glorified in the existence of the works."

—Cat Ellington

166) "Oh shit! I'm in the Urban Dictionary!"
—**Cat Ellington**

167) "I do not point my index finger at anyone lest my thumb should direct itself back towards me. And what I mean by that is this: before I speak about *anything* concerning another person's trials, I will most definitely snatch the curtain back to reveal my own first. Always remember that, my dearest men and women. Because a hypocrite I have never been, nor ever will be. And I'm proud of that fact."
—**Cat Ellington**

168) "I suffered and struggled with morbid obesity as a child. And because of that particular trial, I endured much mistreatment. On one end, I was often attacked, verbally, by bullying people because of my weight, and on the other end, when that trial ended and the massive weight and I parted ways, a different type of animosity from cruel and hateful people broke forth upon me; therefore, I possess a great understanding in the areas of maltreatment."
—**Cat Ellington**

169) "It takes a lot to be one's own person and a leader rather than a group-minded follower. It takes a lot. Individualism is not only powerful but beautiful."
—**Cat Ellington**

170) "Stay in hope. Stay in faith. Stay in love. And keep your joy."

—Cat Ellington

171) "'The Proverbial Diva' is my 'You're So Vain.' Read into the piece whatsoever you will. Read into the piece whatsoever you will."
—**Cat Ellington**

172) "It's just madness, what this pathetic system that needs to constantly fuel the sorry ass engines of low self-esteem, self-hatred, jealousy, false idolatry, and delusional disorder. It's just madness. I honestly cannot think of any other term to describe it."
—**Cat Ellington**

173) "When you see a storm coming towards you, don't turn and run away from it because it'll catch up with you on the same path anyway. But when you see a storm coming towards you, run right through it. Because when you dare to run through a storm, it will eventually pass over you. It will pass, the sun will come out again, and your faith would have been strengthened in the process."
—**Cat Ellington**

174) "While I may often cuss—in heated earthly indignation—I am relentless in my spiritual passion to obey my Lord on this Earth. Truly, I would run the soles off of my feet to obey my Lord's commandments. And He, in His almighty firmament, knows it. Should He command me to walk through a valley of deadly vipers, I would do so in a heartbeat. Because I know that He is not going to allow the venomous fangs of even one to strike me."
—**Cat Ellington**

175) "No one is perfect, we all fall short. But when one knows better, the penalty for him or her will be more severe than for the one who does not know any better."

—**Cat Ellington**

176) "There is simply something amazingly gorgeous about the power of love."
—**Cat Ellington**

177) "The first person who will stick a knife in your back is an ass-kisser, considering that they're already positioned behind you."
—**Cat Ellington**

178) "In the wake of making the good confession, there is always this thing called the 'bliss period.' But once that bliss period ends and a person's trials and tribulations begin, that's when people find out what they're truly made of."
—**Cat Ellington**

179) "It takes an entire community to rebuke a culture of iniquity, and only one given chance to take a life-changing stance."
—**Cat Ellington**

180) "Despite our bumping heads due to any number of our differences, I love Mariah Carey more than any word in the English vocabulary can express. And I would go down fighting for her in a heartbeat if push came to shove. But I will not tolerate her infamous ass Divatude. Not even for a split second."
—**Cat Ellington**

181) "I was the very first person to ever use the tag '6'4 in heels' for my social profile bios. When other women started jumping on it, I decided to let it go as it was not unique anymore."
—**Cat Ellington**

182) "After learning that my name is now a Wheel of Fortune puzzle solution, I am beside myself with humility as the result of this latest blessing."
—**Cat Ellington**

183) "Once upon a time, worldly popularity and I had been quite close. Both it and I were well-acquainted, especially during my teen years into the era of my twenties. Indeed, whithersoever I ventured on land, popularity had its rightful place alongside me as we were inseparable. But on the day that I made the good confession and formed a new, and true, bond of friendship with the Divine Trinity, worldly popularity and I parted ways as it was inevitable."
—**Cat Ellington**

184) "I have to be myself, that's just the way it is. And not everyone is going to understand that."
—**Cat Ellington**

185) "I do not need to strive for social media popularity, it simply isn't important to me. Because I've already *known* popularity. It's not unfamiliar to me."
—**Cat Ellington**

186) "As a professional creative artist in the industry of entertainment, I don't receive money based on likes and followers on any given social media platform. As a professional creative writer in the field of literature, I don't receive money based on likes and followers on any given social media platform."
—**Cat Ellington**

187) "A boat-rocker I can be, yes, but only when I believe that I have been wronged, deliberately, and on more than one occasion."
—**Cat Ellington**

188) "For six years, I have endured much animosity from many people on the social media platform called Twitter. And through it all, I continued onward because I've a job to do. A job that has been in the making for nearly 40 years. And this is the work that brings me joy, what the work that I have been called to do in the arts and entertainment industry. And I make no apologies for it."
—**Cat Ellington**

189) "Power and luxury are not compatible with fools. Always remember that, my dear men and women."
—**Cat Ellington**

190) "I have not done what is evil to any of those men and women who operate Twitter, Inc. But for many years, these have done what is abominably evil to me."
—**Cat Ellington**

191) "I do not apologize for being an African-American woman. I do not apologize for having been born and raised on the South Side of Chicago. I do not apologize for my Pentecostal Christian faith. I do not apologize for the gifts that the Lord has bestowed upon me and implanted within me. I do not apologize for the things that I have earned or received as a result of my many, many years of hard work."
—**Cat Ellington**

192) "We humans are dust, created from the dust of the earth. And as surely as the sun sets itself down at eve, we humans will undoubtedly return to the dust of the earth; therefore, we are not 'superior' one to another."
—**Cat Ellington**

193) "I don't know who submitted my name with a definition to the database of Urban Dictionary, and I don't need to know, it's their business, but I would like to say thank you to whomever he or she may be."
—**Cat Ellington**

194) "John C. Haines elementary school had its student body made up solely of African-American and Chinese children, save for the Galvin siblings who were the only Caucasian kids among us. We were all we had and we loved each other unconditionally."
—**Cat Ellington**

195) "If we Southside kids were nothing else, dammit, we would be highly educated!"

—**Cat Ellington**

196) "Each visitor to the Boutique Domain is unique. My domain provider only counts one IP address at a time. This means that no one, not even myself, can refresh any of its pages in an effort to manipulate the button counter. Only one IP address is tallied at a time. And thus far, there have been over 400,000 of those counted as unique visitors to the Boutique Domain. All organic. No purchased bots, none of that. All true, all genuine. And I am greatly proud of this."
—Cat Ellington

197) "I see social media for exactly what it is: networking. Nothing more, nothing less. But if people are being tempted to view social media platforms as being anything other than what they truly are, or to utilize them to obtain some false and delusional sense of renown—otherwise known as fame—something is wrong with that."
—Cat Ellington

198) "Any lawn of grass can be lush, healthy, and a gorgeous shade of Kelly green if it's well cared for. Therefore, you should nurture your abilities and be at peace. Because once people are tempted to start comparing their own lives to the lives of others, hostilities are sure to arise, especially if they feel inferior or inadequate in comparison to the target of their envy."
—Cat Ellington

199) "Work hard on developing your own skill levels and mind what's on your own plate, not what's on someone else's."

—**Cat Ellington**

200) "Trials and tribulations ain't no sunshiny day at the park. Trust me when I tell you that."
—**Cat Ellington**

201) "I composed 'A Test of Character' while I had been going through a very rough period in my life and felt like my spirit was at the point of breaking altogether. And while that chapter of my life has ended (thank God for blessing me with the strength to have withstood, persevered, and overcome), there are still many of my fellow brethren undergoing their spiritual trials in training for their work that the Lord has chosen for them to do on the Earth. And I want to encourage every one of them to remain at their posts and complete their training. Because I've been there and I know what the barracks are like."
—**Cat Ellington**

202) "There is simply no greater art than that of lovemaking. For it is indeed my most undeniable pleasure, and in it, I take great solace."
—**Cat Ellington**

203) "When one is doing any kind of work in public, especially if that work is considered high-profile, it's best to keep a level head and remember who you are."
—**Cat Ellington**

204) "To those of you out there who can relate to my witness, I say be of good courage and overcome. You're gonna be okay and you're gonna make it. Believe that. You're gonna do just fine. You just watch. All you have to do is reel in that pride and put it in subjection to you. Let go of it and let God handle it."
—**Cat Ellington**

205) "While a wise man will love you for supplying him with a cold drink of sound wisdom, that he should become yet wiser, a scoffer, on the other hand, will gnash his teeth at the truth and hate the one bearing it."

—Cat Ellington

206) "My Southsider would become one with Joseph Strickland's Northsider, and I would at once begin my journey with the man. I would struggle with the man. I would cuss, fuss, and fight with the man. I would laugh a hearty laugh with the man. And I would shed many a bitter tear with the man. Yes, I would make money with the man. I would go broke with the man. I would undergo many trials and tribulations with the man. And I would be greatly blessed with the man. His creative baby had also become my creative baby. And no matter how difficult the trial of carrying the baby was, together, we were going to have our special baby."

—Cat Ellington in *The Making of Dual Mania: Filmmaking Chicago Style* (Vital Vision Publications, 2018)

207) "Upon the completion of filming, our creative baby, 'Dual Mania'—already a high risk conception—collapsed into a coma. In fact, our baby would remain comatose (better than stillborn on any given day, if you ask me) for 17 years. And it was to be a long, stressful ass 17 years."

—Cat Ellington on "Dual Mania"

208) "They all want to see the independent feature film that could, even the same titled 'Dual Mania'!"

—Cat Ellington on "Dual Mania" and the film festival circuit

209) "Live on this Earth long enough and you'll start to notice a pattern, that there is always a price to pay when people are tempted to do evil and be evil."
—**Cat Ellington**

210) "I've always had the following mottos: (1) If you can't speak to me all the time, don't speak to me at all, and (2) If one is not willing to eat beans with you, the same is not worthy to eat steak with you."
—**Cat Ellington**

211) "Since age 10, I have composed hundreds of song works that extend 24 genres."
—**Cat Ellington**

212) "There are many extraordinary and legendary songwriters and composers who have greatly influenced my own style of musical creativity. And whether some of them have passed on or remain with us, their creative contributions continue to play a meaningful role in my own body of work."
—**Cat Ellington**

213) "The idea for the name 'Black Jaguar' was inspired by that particular feline breed while I had been on a class field trip to the Brookfield Zoo in mid April of 1982."
—**Cat Ellington**

214) "I spent countless hours in libraries reading about the music industry, studying it. I craved to know as much as I could about the industry and how it operated, particularly where songwriters were concerned."
—**Cat Ellington**

215) "'Gluttony (The Shell)' is my 'At Seventeen' because the story was inspired by my struggle with childhood obesity, as well as by my having been a very unpopular person among some of the other kids as a result of it."
—**Cat Ellington**

216) "When dealing with people, regardless of whomever they may be, I've always dealt with them straightforwardly. With me, what you see is what you get. Because I don't put on airs. And I'm not a very good liar."
—**Cat Ellington**

217) "If I like you, I'll tell you as much. And I'll tell you exactly why I do, I won't beat around the bush with you. But if I don't like you, trust that I'll tell you as much. And I'll tell you exactly why I don't, I won't beat around the bush with you."
—**Cat Ellington**

218) "After I have extended my hand in a spirit of kindness to anyone, and that person is tempted to regard my hand with spite and hatred, there will never again come a time when I will be willing to extend my hand to the same person. Never again."
—**Cat Ellington**

219) "I'm not willing to kiss anyone's ass and I don't expect anyone to kiss mine."
—**Cat Ellington**

220) "That's the folly with people. They know where they've been, but they don't know where they're going. They can remember what happened yesterday, but they don't know what's going to happen tomorrow. Be careful … for nothing."
—**Cat Ellington**

221) "When categorizing each genre in my song catalog as a 'collection,' being a fashionista also inspired me in regards to the term as it too pays tribute to the fashion industry with its seasonal, uniquely named collections, especially the House of Louis Vuitton with which I have a long-established history as a collector."
—**Cat Ellington**

222) "As much love and admiration as I have for those of my professional fellows within the music industry, particularly those who just so happen to be my main living songwriting influences, it is without a doubt that these extraordinary men and women will nurture a true respect for my musical contributions, no sooner than they are individually released, and regard me, the earthly creator of the same, as one of the most prolific and diverse sole songwriters in the history of the music industry."
—**Cat Ellington**

223) "I tend to call my husband by his last name. I don't call him 'Joe,' I just call him 'Strickland.'"
—**Cat Ellington**

224) "I must honestly say that there was never a time, except once, where we walked into a movie theater in Chicago and had to pay for anything. Strickland's money was never any good in those movie houses because the majority of theater owners knew him. We'd show up at the box office and the ticket agents would just wave us in. We'd help ourselves to the concessions too, free of charge. We never had to pay for

anything in those select theaters: nachos, popcorn, juice, Dots, Raisinettes, you name it."
—**Cat Ellington**

225) "If there's one thing I've learned, it's that the city of Chicago is fanatically obsessed with power."
—**Cat Ellington**

226) "We didn't have any money for a fairy tale wedding, fancy honeymoon, or tiered cake. Every discretionary dollar that we had went towards getting 'Dual Mania' made. Our joint adage was this: 'We can go on a ritzy honeymoon after we have this baby.'"
—Cat Ellington on filmmaker Joseph Strickland

227) "Battling our way through a ton of resistance in the nappy roots of Chicago, we kept the faith (and our joy) through constant prayer, snapping jokes, and going to the movies."
—Cat Ellington on Joseph Strickland and "Dual Mania"

228) "I was learning about a whole new world that I'd previously not known the mechanism of. But in the years that I worked alongside Strickland to transform our baby, 'Dual Mania,' from the script into an actual feature film, I learned quite a bit."
—Cat Ellington

229) "I wanted to keep searching until I found my proper 'Lydia.' And after reviewing dozens and dozens of headshots and résumés from across the country, I came across that beautiful headshot of one Miss Sherrice Eaglin. And on sight, I knew that she was THE 'Lydia' we had been searching for."
—Cat Ellington in *The Making of Dual Mania: Filmmaking Chicago Style* (Vital Vision Publications, 2018)

230) "Everybody ain't asleep. Satan only tries to make it look that way. Everybody ain't lost. Satan only tries to make it look that way. Everybody ain't down and out. Satan only tries to make it look that way."

—Cat Ellington

231) "Whenever you hear someone say, *'In the South Side'* rather than *'On the South Side,'* know for a certainty that the same is an ignorant ass outsider who does not know what the hell he or she is talking about. It's not *'In'* the South Side, dumb-asses, it's *'On'* the South Side."
—**Cat Ellington**

232) "Microchipping, particularly of humans, is the ultimate evil. It is the most atrocious (and inhumane) technology there is, and no one should be deceived—or forced by fear tactics—into undergoing its invasive processes."
—**Cat Ellington**

233) "No sooner had I laid eyes on him and witnessed his audition than I knew he was indeed our 'Tommy Valentine'."
—**Cat Ellington on actor Michael Spitz**

234) "There are badass muthafuckas, and then there's Joseph Strickland – the Scorpio head of his entire domain. He's a greatly blessed soul, and I love him dearly."
—**Cat Ellington**

235) "Wherever we could find available places and spaces to hold our auditions, it had been in those available places and spaces that we held them: at our condo, at Columbia College of Chicago, at fast food restaurants, at the homes of a few performers, at Pizza Hut, at Roosevelt University, at the Signature Room atop the John Hancock building, at Truman College where I'd set up an audition for actress Kiele Sanchez, etc."

—Cat Ellington on casting "Dual Mania"

236) "The performer must—emphasis on must—fit the appropriate look of the character. From there, I present my opinions, or suggestions, to the director, who, of course, would have the final word. So, in my opinion, to some degree, I choose talent over physical beauty – not to say that the two can't co-exist."
—Cat Ellington on casting "Dual Mania"
The Making of Dual Mania: Filmmaking Chicago Style
(Vital Vision Publications, 2018)

237) "It's God's work. The Black Jaguar Music Company, the Centaur Casting Agency, and Quill Pen Ink Publishing are His. I'm just the steward assigned to manage them here on Earth. And I try to do so to the best of my human ability."
—Cat Ellington

238) "I'm not gonna say anything once that I won't be willing to say twice, whether it be over the Internet or face-to-face, whether those to whom I say it be Jews or Gentiles, well-known or unknown, rich and wealthy or poor and needy, dressed in rags or in the finest apparel, blondes, brunettes or redheads, housing project residents or the owners of palatial estates, at the helm of a corporate boardroom table or a member of that same corporation's mail room or janitorial staff, tech company founders and employees or those in the general public who only utilize those companies' social media services, regarded as legends in the entertainment industry or novices within the same. Because my name is on the line, and my word should always be in good standing."

—Cat Ellington

239) "While show business may be cutthroat and full of overly-ambitious hustlers, I still love it to the marrow of my bones."
—Cat Ellington

240) "For as the colored ink from my pen stains my story across the blankness of a white page, it is through my literary witness that I expose what is truth."
—Cat Ellington

241) "This literary witness, divinely inspired as it is, was not intended to be dummied down, negatively influenced, controlled, or mismanaged; but I have an obligation to present the witness in a spirit of fearlessness, boldness, truth, love, and compassion."
—Cat Ellington on her work in literature

242) "The first time I heard the song, a thought entered my mind that said, *Cat, you can write a beautiful song like that.* It was at that moment when I knew I had been given the gift of wisdom to become a writer."
—Cat Ellington on Natalie Cole's "Our Love"

243) "When my right hand starts to itch, regardless of my physical location, I pull out my pen to record the words, particularly for a poem or a review, on a slip of paper. I use my mini recorder to orally record words and melodies if the work is a musical piece and I just so happen to be away from home when I receive it. One cannot choose when the inspiration to write will fall upon them, but they may have a special place where they prefer to compose their works. And in that way, I'm no different. I like to sit in bed with my large keyboard, my notebooks, my pens, my recorder, my coffee, and my bubblegum – you know, all the essentials. And when the creative juices start to flow, I'm all systems go."
—Cat Ellington on songwriting

244) "I have a pooch, a Pomeranian named Aspen. He's a Sagittarius just like me."
—Cat Ellington

245) "I have an insatiable passion for charm bracelets. I love to collect them. Be they vintage or modern, it doesn't matter to me, so long as I have them."
—**Cat Ellington**

246) "I ain't no Venus, Serena, Chris Evert, or Billie Jean King, but I try."
—**Cat Ellington on playing tennis as a hobby**

247) "Interviews last forever. Somewhere, someone will always be able to read them, no matter how much time passes."
—**Cat Ellington**

248) "The style in which I express myself, poetically, is one of appreciable literary inspiration."
—**Cat Ellington**

249) "I mean, I walk around, in the privacy of my home, with my hair all over my head, ya know? I wear a washed face when I'm not out and about, and my nail polish gets chipped, ya know? I'm just Cat. I wear over-sized, holey t-shirts around the house because they're so damn sexy to me and comfy, ya know? And I just don't feel like someone who's famous. I just don't."
—**Cat Ellington**

250) "One to whom much is given, of the same much will be required: for I, myself, have much to lose and far to fall."
—**Cat Ellington**

251) "Part iron and part clay, America is a nation in peril, a divided universe rotating around a bitter-spirited oppressor who cannot obtain a moment's rest unless—or until—he or she has broken the spirit of the oppressed."
—Cat Ellington in her review of James Baldwin's "Another Country"

252) "James Baldwin, in his infinite penmanship, apprehends the madness of the God complex and paints a portrait of spiritual ruination."
—Cat Ellington in her review of James Baldwin's "Another Country"

253) "*Boss: Richard J. Daley of Chicago* is perhaps one of the most phenomenally-written efforts of its respective genre, brandishing a stainless steel weapon of sharp-cutting truth, and dousing the reader with a scalding hot fluid of rage-inducing Godlessness."
—Cat Ellington in her review of Mike Royko's *Boss: Richard J. Daley of Chicago*

254) "A powerful account in the Graphic novel genre, LaMorris Richmond's Boots of the Oppressor is a landmark in its class, a distinction in its own right, and not merely a graphic narrative prepared to suffer from gladness the one who is easily given to swooning."
—Cat Ellington in her review of LaMorris Richmond's "Boots of the Oppressor"

255) "Along Came a Spider is flawless. It is a mesmerizing thriller guaranteed to keep the reader engrossed until the turning of the final page."

—Cat Ellington in her review of James Patterson's "Along Came A Spider"

256) "There is just something special about the literature of the fabled Stephen King. His work, for as long as I have been a reader of it, has always gotten me right here."
—**Cat Ellington**

257) "Michael Eisner is a man that I've always found compelling for some strange reason."
—**Cat Ellington**

258) "'Misery' is bitter cold in both climate and spirit, and ranks at a very high level on the totem pole of King's finest—and most frightening—masterworks."
—**Cat Ellington in her review of Stephen King's "Misery"**

259) "'Cows on Parade' had been a stroke of genius. And many Chicagoans, myself included, cried like newborn babies when the matchless public art exhibit completed its run in our adored city: for we loathed to see them go."
—**Cat Ellington**

260) "When in the city of Chicago, you reserve the right to splurge."
—**Cat Ellington**

261) "It was towards Dolores Price that I felt overcome with such a considerable amount of empathy, what considering that a segmented part of my childhood too included battling the bulge. And I will love her forever, even if only in her fictional existence."
—Cat Ellington on Wally Lamb's "She's Come Undone"

262) "Oh, how dangerous it is to be flesh-minded!"
—Cat Ellington

263) "I cannot even think of the name Carl Hiaasen without chuckling. Because he has that wonderfully distinctive and witty way of combining serious social issues with just the right amount of hilarity."
—Cat Ellington on author Carl Hiaasen

264) "Were his name not credited as this title's author, one would not believe that John Grisham penned 'A Painted House.'"
—Cat Ellington in her review of John Grisham's "A Painted House"

265) "Being a department store, museum, art gallery, and boutique 'historian,' I wanted my place here to mirror those types of establishments in what they will forever represent: style and elegance."
—Cat Ellington on establishing the Boutique Domain

266) "I wore the poor librarians out with my constant inquiries, but I couldn't relent, I had a company to start. And I also had a fiery belly."
—Cat Ellington on establishing Black Jaguar Songs

267) "Rather than having an assemblage of watercolor flowers featured on the covers of the Reviews by Cat Ellington series, Quill Pen Ink Publishing instead commissioned a watercolor graphic showcasing a pair of full lips in an array of bright, vivid colors on a painted black background. In point of fact, the full, painted lips are meant to reflect my very own."
—Cat Ellington on the origin of "Hues of the Reviews"

268) "During the time that I was fifteen, sixteen, seventeen years of age, I would read *Jet* magazine and *Ebony* magazine and fantasize about working for the late, great Eunice W. Johnson and assisting her with the Fashion Fair Cosmetics line."
—Cat Ellington

269) "After a few weeks of brainstorming over memorable names, the idea sprinkled down upon my mental person like refreshing raindrops."
—Cat Ellington on establishing Quill Pen Ink Publishing

270) "Because of my husband, director Joseph Strickland, filmmaking, in its very art form, had become a part of me. I have learned to respect it, admire it, and truly love it. And I

am grateful to now be a member of its professional culture and community."
—**Cat Ellington**

271) "In the perceptions of many people, I, Cat Ellington, am not regarded as someone who is built up in the present system, neither am I regarded as someone who is 'supported' by the corporate structure and mandate, neither am I regarded as someone who has been presented before the people as a 'false idol' for the purpose of worship: for I, Cat Ellington, am not someone who conforms well."
—**Cat Ellington**

272) "A place of being in your shadow is not one appropriate for me, Cat Ellington."
—**Cat Ellington in response to Mariah Carey**

273) "Goodreads is like the Harold Washington Library Center of the Internet. It's exceptional."
—**Cat Ellington**

274) "I love reading books and writing reviews."
—**Cat Ellington**

275) "Though I am a gal who habitually writes in title case, my book reviews are not in title case. Yes, it was tough at first, what typing out my reviews in sentence case, but I eventually got the hang of it."
—**Cat Ellington**

276) "I must let it be known that there has never been a saxophone player I didn't admire strongly."
—**Cat Ellington**

277) "I've been at it, what the craft of songwriting, for over thirty years."
—**Cat Ellington**

278) "I've admired him both as a songwriter and vocalist since the first time I heard 'Plush' back in 1993."
—**Cat Ellington on Scott Weiland**

279) "As one who had been born and raised on Chicago's South Side, I was subjected to a very unique environment where I learned, at a very young age, what it meant to be an African American in this society."
—**Cat Ellington**

280) "I hope that when my productions are finally introduced to the public, either in print or through spoken word performances, those who are not only members of the literary arts community but also lovers of poetry in general will find my writings enjoyable, humorous, educational, intellectual, exciting, awe-inspiring, and even thought-provoking."
—**Cat Ellington**

281) "The greatest canvas in the world is the city of Chicago. And I'll go to my grave with that."
—**Cat Ellington**

282) "I wish I could have assisted with the composition of this work, that's how deeply in love with it I am."
—**Cat Ellington on Herb Alpert's "This Guy's In Love With You"**

283) "Oh, how I love greatness! Like the kind of greatness Hitch had undoubtedly been in his day."
—**Cat Ellington on director Alfred Hitchcock**

284) "The Lord had been with His daughter here on His Earth, and she is now with Him at Home in His glorious Kingdom."
—**Cat Ellington on the death of Aretha Franklin**

285) "The color-coded cover art for each individual volume in the entire anthological series of Reviews by Cat Ellington has been graced with its very own unique identity. And I am over the moon with excitement because it's a dream come true."
—**Cat Ellington on "Hues of the Reviews"**

286) "Honestly, if I weren't married to Joseph Strickland, I would most definitely be married to Jesse L. Martin."
—**Cat Ellington**

287) "I'm a one-woman show in all three of my creative houses."
—**Cat Ellington**

288) "I've no time for, neither do I give a damn about, people who are full of low self-esteem, self-hatred, rage, racism, anger, envy, jealousy, bitterness, malice, fear, or any other kind of negative resentment towards me."
—**Cat Ellington**

289) "I am not one who goes through life bearing false witness against others, neither are stupidity and gullibility my strong suits."
—**Cat Ellington**

290) "His depiction will never be rivaled – I don't care what anyone says."
—**Cat Ellington on Heath Ledger in his portrayal of the "Joker"**

291) "A great voice, and a great songwriting talent."
—Cat Ellington on Bill Withers

292) "A cinematic masterpiece if there ever was one. I love this film with everything I have."
—Cat Ellington on Stanley Kubrick's *2001: A Space Odyssey*

293) "No other act in music can perform 'Riders On The Storm' the way Jimmy and the boys did."
—Cat Ellington on The Doors

294) "He was one of the most handsome, not to mention incredibly gifted, men that ever lived."
—Cat Ellington on Curtis Mayfield

295) "I love…well, I love greatness. And my fellow Southsider, Max Sansing? Well, he's greatness."
—Cat Ellington on famed Chicago muralist, Max Sansing

296) "I'm like a black diamond, I shine ever so brightly."
—**Cat Ellington**

297) "The false mask. The false face. The false adoration. The false words spoken. The false idolatry. These are the lying things that the aforementioned see and hear. But to me, the true face is revealed: racism, bigotry, hatred, envy, jealousy, lust, anger, bitterness, self-hatred, low self-esteem, malice, revenge, and rage."
—**Cat Ellington in reaction to Twitter**

298) "This is the Boutique Domain, my place. And here, I speak freely. No one can lock me out here, especially for no reason. The Black Jaguar Music Company pays for this location to operate. And should the Black Jaguar Music Company choose to cease its financing, well, I reckon that the Boutique Domain will be no longer."
—**Cat Ellington at the Boutique Domain, in response to an unwarranted Twitter account suspension**

299) "I am a woman of my true word."
—**Cat Ellington**

300) "The leisure of reading has lost its luster, as many members of this generation have become absorbed in, even obsessed with, technology, be its form social media, game apps, or what have you. Associates of that specific group are simply unfocused. And then you have others who just can't be bothered to sit down and relax with a really good book

that they may truly enjoy, too overwhelmed with the distractions of daily living."

—Cat Ellington in an interview with The IndieView

301) "Hey, Stephen King didn't get to be Stephen King by sitting around being faithless. The great man, gifted with vast literary wisdom, put the work in, and then closed in on the old school brick-and-mortar publishing houses of New York to get his chilling stories read by millions."
—**Cat Ellington**

302) "It's coming to a point where reading a novel of fiction (or even nonfiction) will be considered a luxury rather than a basic hobby."
—**Cat Ellington**

303) "Overall, I don't believe that reading as a pastime is dying as there will always be bookworms who populate the earth in considerable numbers. Authors will continue onward in their crafts of creating exciting stories, and there will be book lovers the world over who will support their creative contributions."
—**Cat Ellington**

304) "My primary careers are in the entertainment industry! This means that I am completely accustomed to drama…of every varietal. Strife is strife – be it in show business or literature."
—**Cat Ellington**

305) "There are reviewers out there who would not be so welcoming of an irate author, except that I am not one of them."
—**Cat Ellington**

306) "Where the rating system is concerned, greatness is in the eye of the reader."
—Cat Ellington in her capacity as a professional book reviewer

307) "Grammatical errors, that can be corrected in edited reissues, ought not be considered if a novel is five-star worthy in both plot and character development."
—Cat Ellington

308) "For even some who look like me, according to the pigmentation of the flesh, are the same who strive to deny my God-given abilities. That is a form of racism, wrapped up in inferiority complexes."
—Cat Ellington

309) "Contrary to popular belief, White people don't have a monopoly on the spirit of racism."
—Cat Ellington

310) "The elements are alive and free. They don't love and they don't hate, they just wash away the old to make room for the new."
—Cat Ellington

311) "My soul is hugged and kissed by art."
—**Cat Ellington**

312) "Much like with ASCAP, as a songwriter, in 2003, and the Academy of American Poets, as a poet, in 2013, my joining the Authors Guild, as an author, in 2020 is a childhood dream come true."
—**Cat Ellington**

313) "One of Joe Strickland's and my favorite movies of all time. I swear, we never, ever get tired of it."
—**Cat Ellington on "The Thomas Crown Affair" (1999)**

314) "Since the time that I was old enough to remember, my mother had never ceased to share with me the following wisdom: 'Always watch how you treat people because you never know how God is coming.'"
—**Cat Ellington**

315) "It's a classic film. Even. To. This. Day. Fascinating cinematography!"
—**Cat Ellington on Spike Lee's "Malcolm X"**

316) "I honestly don't believe that there's any other actor who could portray 'Agent Smith' the way he did. His overall depiction was flawless!"
—Cat Ellington on actor Hugo Weaving

317) "Truly, she had been one of the greatest femme fatales to ever grace the timeless film noir genre. And I never get tired of watching her perform on screen."
—Cat Ellington on screen legend Linda Darnell

318) "My life is now being filtered through the public eye: what I do, what I say, where I go. If I were to say, get caught stealing a pressed powder compact, chances are that it'll make news once the authorities learn my identity and what I do for a living."
—Cat Ellington on being a public figure

319) "I would kindly advise anyone who may take up an interest in catcalling me to be well-prepared for a fun-filled, and sometimes dizzying, verbal adventure that I will surely take them on, if I so choose to answer his or her call."
—Cat Ellington

320) "The written word. It is my power."
—Cat Ellington

321) "The U.S. Marines don't play! Like the Navy SEALs, they will tear yo' ass up! Love the Marines! Love the U.S. Armed Forces, period, but especially them and the SEALs."
—**Cat Ellington**

322) "There is absolutely nothing wrong with any woman having plastic surgery if it is what would make her feel more vibrant, sexy, youthful, or otherwise."
—**Cat Ellington**

323) "I'm anemic. And I strive to remain vigilant where my daily dose of blackstrap molasses is concerned."
—**Cat Ellington**

324) "There's just something about the long e sound. I don't know what. Maybe it has to do with that particular sound being among one of the first that I learned in my nearly thirty-five-years-long written vocabulary history."
—**Cat Ellington**

325) "I have to watch my weight because my metabolism ain't worth a damn."
—**Cat Ellington**

326) "Grace Kelly's 'Lisa Carol Fremont' is my spirit animal."

—Cat Ellington

327) "Terrence Malick is an exceptional filmmaker, period. His creative vision is awe-inspiring."

—Cat Ellington

328) "Creativity is one of my most beloved things in the whole wide world!"

—Cat Ellington

329) "The arts community in Chicago is never short of artists bursting with uniquely creative ideas."

—Cat Ellington

330) "Faith is a beautiful thing. And so is hope."

—Cat Ellington

331) "Songwriters are the salt of the Earth."

—Cat Ellington

This has been a presentation of quotes by Cat Ellington.
Thank you for viewing.

Coming Soon

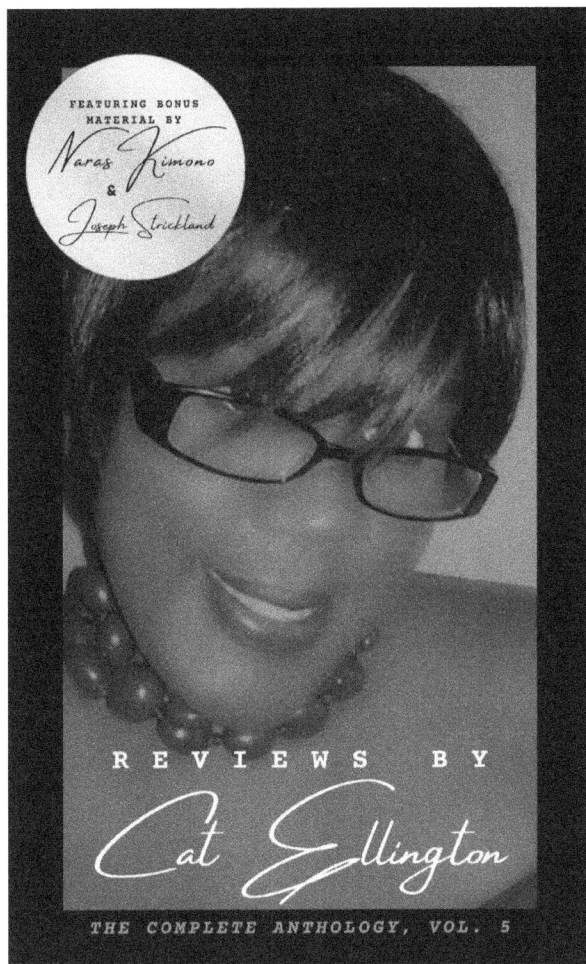

Reviews by Cat Ellington: The Complete Anthology, Vol. 5
Cover Hue: Ultraviolet

About the Author

Cat Ellington is an American songwriter, casting director, poet, and author from Chicago, IL. She is best known for her creative contributions to the diverse industries and fields of music, movies, art, and literature.

Outside of her professional element, the award-winning lyricist enjoys reading, listening to music, cooking, collecting vintage and modern charm bracelets, watching LMN, film noir movies, and classic TV shows, sailing, jet skiing, playing tennis, and eating lots of frozen yogurt.

Cat Ellington lives in Chicago with her husband Joseph Strickland, their three children Nathaniel, Nairobi, and Naras, and the family's pet Pomeranian, Aspen.

Cat Ellington on Amazon: Books,
Biography, Blog, Audiobooks, Kindle

Cat Ellington at the Award-Winning
Boutique Domain

Cat Ellington at the Review Period with
Cat Ellington

Cat Ellington at IMDb

www.ingramcontent.com/pod-product-compliance
Lightning Source LLC
Chambersburg PA
CBHW022120280326
41933CB00007B/477